Original title:
The Pear's Treasure

Copyright © 2025 Creative Arts Management OÜ
All rights reserved.

Author: Henry Beaumont
ISBN HARDBACK: 978-1-80586-402-8
ISBN PAPERBACK: 978-1-80586-874-3

Unspoken Joys Hidden Amongst the Foliage

Among the leaves, quite green and bright,
A treasure waits, just out of sight.
With giggles masked, the critters play,
They find the joy in every day.

Beneath the branches, secrets creep,
While squirrels dance and chipmunks leap.
A playful breeze, a rustling sound,
In hidden spots, fun can be found.

Abundance Encased in Lushness

In gardens lush, with colors bold,
Lies hidden wealth—not made of gold.
With leaves that tickle and shadows that tease,
Nature's bounty brings smiles with ease.

Laughing bugs on a swinging vine,
In every nook, joy intertwines.
Round and ripe, the fruits all grin,
A feast of fun that draws us in.

The Sweetness of Forgotten Harvests

Long since past, the harvests smile,
With stories sweet, they stretch a mile.
Lost in time, their flavors bloom,
They whisper tales in every room.

A fruity jest, an unexpected bite,
Who knew such joy could be so bright?
With every nibble, laughter flows,
In memories sweet, the fun just grows.

Wonders Wrapped in Nature's Embrace

Beneath the sky where laughter sways,
Nature holds its fun-filled ways.
With wrinkled smiles and roots that twine,
Every moment's a joyful line.

The sun peeks through with cheeky gleams,
In leafy greens, we chase our dreams.
Each step unveils a giggling plot,
Nature's wonders, a happy lot.

Enigmatic Abundance of the Orchard

In the orchard where fruits play,
A pear thought it could ballet.
With a twist and a spin,
It fell with a grin—

An apple watched, said, 'Oh dear!'
'Your dance is absurd, I fear.'
But with laughter anew,
The pear flew off, too!

A bunch of fruits joined the spree,
Bananas giggled with glee.
The tree swayed with mirth,
What a joyous rebirth!

So here in this quirky delight,
Fruits frolic, a wonderful sight.
In this garden of cheer,
There's magic quite near!

The Symphony of Sugary Secrets

A sweet tune wafted so clear,
Fruits gathered to lend an ear.
Oh, what a delight,
In moon's soft light!

The berries formed quite a band,
With grapefruits clapping their hands.
The pears hummed along,
In the fruit choir strong.

A coconut's knock on the shell,
Drew laughter, you could tell.
As cherries swayed in glee,
What a sight to see!

With each rhythm and rhyme,
They danced on the vine,
In this sugary groove,
Nothing left to prove!

Sweet Secrets in Green Hollows

In the orchard where whispers roam,
Fruits giggle, feeling right at home.
Chasing bees with silly glee,
Twirling leaves in jubilee.

Moonlight winks through branches wide,
Jokes endure where flavors hide.
A cheeky breeze starts a chat,
Buds reveal where fun is at.

Beneath the Luscious Skin

Peel back laughter, taste the zest,
Underneath, there's quite a jest.
Each bite's a riddle, sweet and strong,
With juice that sings a fruity song.

Exploring flavors, twist and twirl,
Fruitful giggles start to swirl.
Juicy tales and flavors mix,
Who knew a snack could play such tricks?

Gems in the Gnarled Tree

Nestled high in branches stout,
Gems of laughter dance about.
Squirrels swing with acrobatic flair,
Chasing riches that float in air.

With each pluck, a chuckle grows,
Nature's bounty, oh, it shows!
In the hollow, treasures gleam,
Making mischief a daily dream.

Nectar's Unfolding

In the morning, sweetness wakes,
Nectar spills for tasty shakes.
Buzzing bees hum lighthearted tunes,
As blossoms strut in sunny afternoons.

Laughter drips from vibrant blooms,
Joy hides anywhere it zooms.
Sip the fun that life bestows,
Fruity giggles in every dose.

Sweet Abundance Revealed

In a garden lush with cheer,
A fruit drops, enticing near.
Bouncing round with such a grin,
Its hidden prize tucked underneath skin.

Jokes aside, it surely gleams,
In salads or in silly dreams.
Wiggly worms start to prance,
Admiring every juicy chance.

With bites of sweetness, giggles sprout,
As friends all gather 'round to pout.
"Did you see that? It just rolled!"
There's laughter in this fruit so bold.

Funny facts, its seeds are few,
But cheerfulness will grow anew.
In each slice, joy on display,
A fruity riddle, come what may!

Shadows of the Fruity Enigma

Beneath the shade where shadows play,
A mystery grows, come join the fray.
Its curves are round, its color bright,
A puzzling fruit, such pure delight.

With winks and giggles, children gaze,
At how it's ripened in sun's rays.
They guess its name, but oh, the plight!
It's only known at lunchtime bite!

Whispers swirl of flavors bold,
Sweet secrets from the orchard told.
With every crunch, the laughter flows,
As silly stories bubble, who knows?

Dancing ants trail along the ground,
Trying to see what's all around.
In every bite, a jest awaits,
The fruity life, oh, how it flirts!

Golden Curves of Delight

A golden orb hangs from its tree,
Its shape is round, so full of glee.
With every stumble, laughs abound,
As the harvest spills upon the ground.

Bright and cheerful, a sight to see,
This fruity wonder, come taste with me.
It rolls away, what a silly caper,
Chasing joy, like a much-loved paper.

Friends gather 'round for a tasting spree,
Each bite brings jokes as tasty as can be.
"Is it a globe or a hidden prize?"
They grin with mischief in their eyes.

What's hidden inside, is it treasure rare?
A burst of goodness, beyond compare.
In every slice, smiles must sprout,
Crisp laughter echoes, there's no doubt!

The Essence of Orchard Mystique

In orchards where secrets often play,
Wonders grow throughout the day.
Mischief waits in every leaf,
A burst of joy beyond belief.

With silly hats and fruit-filled games,
This fruity enigma has no claims.
With giggles ringing by every tree,
Each bite brings forth a laugh so free.

As summer breezes, tales take flight,
With vibrant shades, oh, what a sight!
Beneath the branches, humor flows,
In fruity whispers, the laughter grows.

So take a bite, embrace the cheer,
Let's celebrate this time of year.
In every taste, the jokes will bloom,
Within these fruits, we'll find our room!

Nectar of Forgotten Dreams

In a grove where dreams collide,
A funny fruit swings side to side.
Giggling winds share silly tales,
Bouncing laughter, nature's gales.

Rustling leaves whisper a cheer,
As quirky critters come near.
One plump pear dons a goofy grin,
Enticing all to join the spin.

Sweet nectar drips from leafy seams,
Laughter blooms in sunlit beams.
Who knew a fruit could juggle fun,
In this silly dance, we've all won!

Buried Riches Amongst the Branches

High in limbs where secrets hide,
Silly treasures, slyly tied.
Roots that chuckle, branches tease,
Hidden gems, they aim to please.

Oh, a sock, a hat, and a shoe,
All buried 'neath the fruit we knew.
"What a find!" the critters shout,
Such priceless riches all about!

Beneath the pear, a world of jest,
Where every find becomes a quest.
With giggles bouncing in the air,
Digging treasures everywhere!

A Legacy of Green and Gold

In fields of green and yellow hue,
Silly stories sprout anew.
A legacy of giggles growing,
This merry clan keeps on glowing.

From fruit of gold to greens so bright,
Each laughs, sprouting pure delight.
Amidst the harvest, there's surprise,
As laughter gleams from every size.

With every slice a grin appears,
The sweetest moments, shared with cheers.
Seeds of joy in every fold,
This legacy is pure and bold!

Enigmas of the Fruitful Grove

In the grove, where puzzles dwell,
A fruity riddle casts a spell.
Round and plump with a dandy glare,
A fruity secret kept with care.

What sings at dusk and glows by dawn?
The curious fruits thrive on and on.
With every mystery, laughter grows,
In the grove, anything goes!

Giggling trees and dancing vines,
Join the antics with silly signs.
In the heart of nature's cheer,
The enigmas draw us ever near!

Beneath the Weight of the Branches

Underneath the boughs, I spy,
Fruits that dangle, oh so high.
They wiggle, wobble, tease my reach,
A game of stretch, a fruit-filled breach.

The squirrels debate, "Is it our turn?"
While I plot and twist, my fingers yearn.
With every leap, a dance of fate,
Soon I'll taste, but first—can I wait?

A thud, a giggle, a curious crow,
Makes me tumble, putting on quite a show.
As laughter echoes, the breeze does play,
In the orchard's heart, we're all child's play.

So here beneath the branches stout,
Life's a circus—there's no doubt!
With every bite, a moment grand,
Sharing joy while fruits withstand.

Radiance Draped in Leaves

Among the leaves, a glimmer shines,
Gold and green, like precious signs.
They peek and hide, a cheeky tease,
These glowing gems sway in the breeze.

Each day I ponder, which to pick,
Tugging the branches, trying a trick.
A fruit that rolls, I chase with glee,
Like playful fairies, it runs from me.

Flavors burst like laughter bright,
With each sweet bite, a new delight.
The giggles mix with fruity zest,
Under the sun, we're nature's jest.

So here we laugh, 'neath leaves so lush,
In this orchard, there's never a rush.
With every crunch, joy's little art,
And in the fruit, we'll find our heart.

The Silence of Ripening Fruits

In stillness waits a hopeful crew,
Shhh, don't tell them, they don't have a clue!
With every tick of time, they grow,
Fruity whispers floating, a soft glow.

They giggle as the sunbeam winks,
Plotting sweetness, oh, what a jinx!
With every breeze, a little dance,
Nature's jesters, ready to prance.

Alas! A critter inches near,
With hungry eyes—a little sneer.
The fruits just sigh, "Not yet, not yet!"
In ripening silence, we place our bet.

So hush the orchard, let them be,
With secret smiles, just wait and see.
When the moment's right, they'll make a fuss,
Then berries burst, and laughter's a must!

Arcane Secrets of the Orchard

In shadows deep, old tales are spun,
Orchard whispers under the sun.
Mystic fruits of oddest hue,
Guarding secrets both old and new.

I spy a pear that wears a hat,
Winking like a jolly cat.
Its secrets hidden, tucked away,
It giggles softly, come what may.

The apples chat in colors bright,
Sharing gossip till the night.
With each bite taken, stories swell,
In every crunch, a secret spell.

So romp and roll, embrace this lore,
In every fruit, there's something more.
With laughter, joy, and silly schemes,
The orchard holds our sweetest dreams.

Sweet Reflections in Orchard Light

In the orchard where laughter grows,
Fruit dangles like jokes in rows.
Sunshine tickles the leaves' green,
A fruity giggle—is that a scene?

Hanging low, they wink and sway,
Whispers of sweetness come out to play.
Who knew fruit could be so sly?
The juiciest tricks catch a passerby!

Each bite's a chuckle, full of glee,
A fruit-filled ride to jubilee.
Sun-kissed humor and fruity delight,
In every scoop, laughter takes flight.

With each pluck, a pun does rise,
They crack us up in fuzzy guise.
So come on down, don't be a tease,
In this orchard, everyone leaves with ease!

Mysteries Wrapped in Juicy Flesh

A round and plump enigma hides,
With skins so bright, they play with tides.
Taste a riddle, juicy and sly,
Each bite invites a giggle or cry.

Underneath that sun-kissed peel,
Lies the secret—sweet and surreal.
You bite in deep, a whoopee cushion,
Oops! That laughter? Just a sweet intrusion!

Fruits play tricks, that's their game,
Like sneaky kids who can't be named.
Peeling back layers, a mystery bursts,
Juicy revelations, all quenched thirsts.

In laughter's court, these fruits hold sway,
With every mouthful, don't waste the day!
Pleased to report, juicy worlds confound,
Each fruity joke leaves you spellbound!

Lush Secrets of Summer's Lure

Bright blooms call, in vibrant cheer,
Whispers of summer, drawing near.
Among the branches, giggles twine,
Each luscious secret tastes divine.

Surprises sneak through every bite,
Jumping flavors, a wild flight.
They play peek-a-boo, oh so bold,
In the sunshine, their stories unfold!

Round and happy, the fruits do dance,
A juicy jig, a merry prance.
So grab a few, don't hold back,
These lush delights are on the attack!

They'll tickle your taste buds, make you sigh,
With every munch, you'll surely fly.
Caught in summer's playful tease,
These fruits serve joy like a cool breeze!

Harvest Dreams Bursting with Flavor

Fields abound with heavenly sights,
Fruits compete in dazzling lights.
Each harvest morning brings delight,
Chasing senses, what a sight!

Laughing fruits, they vie for fame,
Charming smiles, they play their game.
Biting in brings a happy surprise,
Flavors dancing, none can disguise!

From trees like dreams, they tumble down,
No frowning faces in this town.
Every scoop, a burst of cheer,
Harvest joy, oh so near!

Join the feast, it's such a bliss,
Sweet laughter lives in every kiss.
Ripe and ready, gleeful and bold,
These fruity dreams are pure gold!

The Bounty Beneath the Canopy

Beneath the leaves, a secret stirred,
Tiny critters danced and chirped,
A fruit so round, so shiny and bold,
Its sweetness, a story yet untold.

The squirrels plot, they scurry and race,
For the prize that's found in this leafy place,
They tackle each other, no holds barred,
For a taste of the fruit that stands on guard.

With laughter loud, their antics display,
The chase for treasure brightens the day,
But up in the branches, a grinning bird,
Watches the circus without a word.

As daylight fades, their fuss turns sweet,
One slips and falls — a comical feat!
Yet when they pair up, they find delight,
In the Bounty's glow, round and bright!

Autumn's Prized Offerings

In crisp fall air, a gathering's begun,
With laughs and tunes, all vying for fun,
Gather 'round folks, with plates piled high,
With laughter echoing beneath the sky.

A plump contender, rolled on the ground,
Tumbles and bumbles, with a merry sound,
Slip and slide, all covered in leaves,
The chase for bounty that autumn weaves.

Here comes a dog, all wagging and wild,
Chasing new snacks like a playful child,
With wagging tail, he's leading the game,
For the prized offerings, none are the same.

And when the sun sets, this festive cheer,
Leaves golden memories to hold dear,
With smiles and giggles, the harvest ends,
In laughter's echo, nature transcends!

Nature's Unseen Abundance

In shadows deep, a giggle hides,
Beneath the branches where mischief abides,
A plump surprise lays low in the grass,
While unsuspecting critters just pass.

A sneaky glance, a rustle, a thud,
Nature's treasure becomes a big flood,
Chasing each other, they tumble and fall,
Unseen abundance, amusement for all.

Beneath the bush, a pair plots away,
For the bright orb, 'tis the game they play,
With slappy little feet and tiny cries,
Chasing the sun, it's a comical rise.

Amidst the fun, laughter rings clear,
Nature's delight supplies the cheer,
A bounty unseen, but felt all around,
Where joy and giggles in chaos abound!

Dreams Cradled in Green

In gardens bright, where dreams unfold,
The leafy whispers have stories told,
With cheeky grins, the critters conspire,
To pluck the dreams, their hearts ever higher.

Each twirl and flap, they dance and leap,
Through rows of green, their secrets keep,
A hidden laughter in every touch,
The sweet reward makes it all such fun.

With bright colors, the scene's a jest,
As laughter carries, they never rest,
A chase for delight, what a jabberwock!
In dreams of green, they learn to talk.

As daylight dims and shadows sway,
They chuckle soft, content in play,
For the dreams they cradle, oh so sweet,
In nature's embrace, they find their beat!

Secrets Unfurled in Sun-Kissed Fields

In a field so bright and wide,
A pear once tried to hide inside.
But laughter echoed from the tree,
"You can't be quiet, come dance with me!"

The rabbits giggled, hopping near,
While squirrels whispered, full of cheer.
"A pear in disguise? What a sight!"
They rolled with laughter, pure delight.

Sunset painted skies with glee,
As giggles bounced from leaf to tree.
A treasure found beneath the sun,
In fields where laughter's just begun.

So if you wander, take a look,
For secrets hide in every nook.
Where nature's wisdom laughs and plays,
In sun-kissed fields, where joy always stays.

Beneath the Skin of Nature's Blessings

Beneath the surface, funny things,
A pear was grinning, sprouting wings.
With all its friends, a fruit parade,
Beneath the leaves, a grand charade!

The apples chuckled, 'What a sight!
A pear with wings, oh what a flight!'
They rolled their eyes as they would say,
'Our pear's a fruit that's gone astray!'

Dancing daisies joined the fun,
While bread-and-circus grabbed a bun.
Under the sun, beneath the trees,
They laughed and played with every breeze.

Oh nature's riddle holds delight,
Where pears with wings take joyful flight.
Beneath the skin of all that's grown,
Lies laughter shared, and fun well-known.

Sweet Recollections of Orchard Tales

In orchards lush, where stories bloom,
A pear once claimed a corner gloom.
"I'm not just fruit, I'm fun and rhyme!"
It jingled softly, keeping time.

The cherries rolled their little eyes,
"A pear that jives? Now that's a prize!"
They danced along in pure delight,
Igniting laughter, oh what a sight!

With each sweet tale of days gone by,
The winds would giggle, trees would sigh.
In every bite, a jest, a cheer,
Reminders to hold laughter dear.

So gather 'round, young and the old,
For stories sweet and jokes retold.
In orchards rich with tales of glee,
A pear's true magic, wild and free.

The Silent Symphony of the Fruits

In shady groves of vibrant hues,
A pear was muted, not a muse.
But all its friends, both small and bright,
Played symphonies, oh what a sight!

The grapes would mouth a silent tune,
While apples hummed beneath the moon.
"Your silence is a funny act!"
The pear rolled red, a joyful fact.

With hushed tones, fruits learned to sway,
Creating rhythms, bright as day.
Though one remained in quiet bliss,
Its inner giggle led to this!

A symphony in silent plays,
With fruits engaging in witty ways.
For even fruits can laugh and cheer,
In joyous dances, year by year.

Whispers of Juicy Gold

In a garden where laughter grows,
Little critters in tidy rows.
They plot and scheme for a sweet delight,
Chasing fruit under the moonlight.

A squirrel dons a tiny hat,
Claiming riches from where he sat.
The breeze dances through every tree,
Echoing whispers of glee and glee.

Belly laughs from the plump old bear,
Stumbling over roots laid bare.
Said a crow with a knowing wink,
'Better share before we sink!'

They giggle at a juicy jest,
Each bite savored, surely the best!
In jest and juice, they find surprise,
With sticky paws and cheerful eyes.

Secrets Beneath the Leaf

Under leaves where shadows lie,
A rabbit dreams with a crooked sigh.
'What's hidden here, oh, so divine?'
Mysteries flow like vintage wine.

The beetles dance, with great finesse,
Wearing shiny coats, they impress.
They whisper tales of plump delight,
While munching greens in the pale light.

A ladybug joins the silly game,
Bragging about her colorful fame.
'I've seen fruits that would make you weep!'
As they giggle, not a peep!

A treasure map, so cleverly drawn,
But all their plans are nearly gone.
For laughter echoes, what's out of sight,
Is just a slice, shared with delight.

The Orchard's Hidden Bounty

In the orchard where mischief thrives,
The fruit flies tell of secret dives.
A trio of thieves, oh what a sight,
With fuzzy faces, they giggle and bite.

Danny the dog, with a wagging tail,
Chased after dreams, but always would fail.
'Why chase the wind when fruits abound?'
He howls with joy, hopping around.

A cat in shades, with a cool demean,
Steals the scene like it's all a game.
'You'll never catch me, just watch and see!'
With laughter bubbles, all agree.

Hidden bounties beneath the sun,
With every giggle, they steal a run.
An orchard of fun, they cheer, they play,
In fruity worlds, they find the way.

A Harvest of Delicate Dreams

When morning dawns and winks at dawn,
The critters dance upon the lawn.
Harvest dreams wrapped up in glee,
Wandering where the sweet things be.

A dance of butterflies, oh so fair,
Sipping nectar, without a care.
A joke exchanged among the bees,
Buzzing puns carried on the breeze.

Plump cherries start a hasty race,
Rolling down with a fruity grace.
'Catch me if you can!' they tease and twirl,
While the dew drops shine and unfurl.

In every giggle, there's magic spun,
A harvest of laughter, pure fun begun.
With every turn, there's joy, it seems,
In nature's bounty, we find our dreams.

Secrets Sown in Fertile Soil

In gardens bright, a plot was laid,
With seeds of laughter, mischief played.
A sprout so round, it dressed in green,
It rolled away, where had it been?

With roots that wink, and leaves that cheer,
It danced about, no hint of fear.
The critters laughed, they joined the fun,
In fields where puns were overrun.

Each morning bright, it teased the sun,
But with a twist, it wouldn't run.
For every mile it tried to glide,
It found a way to slip and slide.

In soil that giggled, nature's jest,
A harvest of chuckles, the very best.
With every bloom, the fun would grow,
Unruly greens, putting on a show.

Glimmers of Sweetness in Sunlight

A splash of gold, so round and bright,
Beneath the sun, it felt just right.
It pranced along the garden bed,
With juicy dreams dancing in its head.

The bumblebees formed quite the crew,
Buzzing tunes as they flew through.
Their pollen parties made a scene,
With laughter sprouting in between.

As ants discussed the day's huge score,
They claimed the prize, the sweetest ore.
In every leaf, a giggle grows,
A circus act, as sweetness flows.

With sunlight's kiss, it feels so grand,
Each glimmer winks, a playful hand.
In nature's joke, we find our glee,
In every bite, pure jubilee.

Whispers of Nature's Gift

In secret chats, the vines conspire,
With whispers soft, they never tire.
A fruity plot in leafy shade,
Where jokes are cracked and pals are made.

The squirrels joke, "What will we munch?"
As they prepare for their next crunch.
Each nibble tells a tale or two,
In nature's club, the fun's in view.

The wind would giggle, shake the leaves,
Unraveling tales the garden weaves.
Where every thorn holds laughter dear,
A prickly jest brings smiles near.

With treasures sweet and humor spry,
Nature's gift waves us on by.
A secret stash in every bite,
Where joy and leaves intertwine tight.

The Allure of the Ripe Harvest

A harvest time, oh what a sight,
With colors bold, a feast so bright.
Each fruit a wink, a playful tease,
In baskets stacked, no room to squeeze.

The pickers laughed, their hands all stained,
With juicy smudges, they were gained.
"Let's race the cart!" they shouted loud,
As nature chuckled, feeling proud.

The pumpkins rolled, the berries sang,
In autumn's air, the joy just sprang.
With every grab, a funny slip,
As laughter flowed, they'd take a trip.

Each moment shared, a memory sown,
In laughter framed, they felt at home.
With every bite, the fun would last,
And joyful harvests raised the glass.

Boundless Joys of Autumn's Gift

In the orchard, laughter rings,
Bouncing fruit from playful swings.
Joyful giggles fill the air,
As we chase those golden pear.

Tumbling, rolling, round they go,
With buttery smiles that steal the show.
Silly dances in the sun,
A fruity contest, who had the most fun?

In baskets piled, our prizes gleam,
But sticky fingers? What a theme!
With every bite, more giggles spring,
Autumn's delight is a tasty thing.

So grab a friend, join in the cheer,
Let's savor the sweetness, spread the merry here!
In this orchard, life's lush feast,
A whimsical world where joy won't cease.

Rustling Leaves, Whispered Treasures

Leaves are murmuring secrets sweet,
Underfoot they rustle, crisp and neat.
Hidden jewels, beneath the trees,
Each step reveals a fun surprise, if you please!

Wind whispers jokes through limbs so wide,
With gales that giggle and misguide.
Bouncing fruits, oh what a sight,
As we stumble, laughing with delight.

Fruits in colors, red, green, and gold,
Each a promise of stories untold.
Who knew just one sight would please?
A comical chase in the autumn breeze!

In this maze of nature's jest,
Who knew pears could be such a quest?
Harvest laughter, don't let it slip,
For in each bite, a playful trip!

Enigma of the Orchard's Heart

What's hidden in the boughs so high?
The secret laughter, oh, my-oh-my!
Chasing shadows, we trip and fall,
Each stumble leads to fruity brawl!

The mystery ripens in every nook,
Just a peek? Oh, take a look!
Bubbles in cider, laughter's the theme,
Join the fun, live the dream!

The trees, they chuckle, sway and bow,
What fun they have, seeming to know how.
Nature's riddle, a giggle away,
Let's unravel tales in a joyous play!

As laughter flows like a bubbling stream,
In this orchard, life's the dream.
So swipe a pear, hoard the glee,
In this funny riddle, come and be free!

The Dance of Sweetness and Sun

Sunlight sparkles on dew-kissed leaves,
Nature's boogie, oh how it weaves!
Swaying fruits, a jolly sight,
Twisting in turns, what pure delight!

Pears and laughter, vibrant embrace,
Join the frolic, quicken the pace!
Tickling branches, sweet and bright,
Twirl with joy from morning's light.

The sun spills honey, over the hill,
We giggle together, odder still.
Each dance a treasure, each twirl a thrill,
In this orchard, there's laughter to fill!

So grab a friend, let's sway and prance,
Celebrate autumn with a funny dance!
For in this harvest, joy takes flight,
In a jestful world, everything's right!

Harvest Moon and Juicy Secrets

Under the harvest moon so bright,
Fruits giggle in the pale moonlight.
A pear in a hat, what a sight,
Drinking cider, feeling light.

They gossip of the juiciest day,
Ripening in a comical way.
With each bite, laughter will sway,
Tasting secrets, come what may.

Neighbors peek, their eyes aglow,
Wondering what we all know.
A dance of flavors, quite the show,
In the orchard, seeds will sow.

Underneath the stars we play,
Making fun of every spray.
Witty puns lead the way,
In this fruit-filled grand buffet!

The Elixir of Autumn's Hand

What's in that bubbling cauldron, oh?
A hint of spice and giggles flow.
Whispers of apples, a cheeky show,
As pears toss leaves like confetti go.

Autumn's hand is full of zest,
Mixing flavors, as they jest.
With every sip, we feel blessed,
Laughter brewing, quite the fest!

Sipping cider, we take a chance,
A dance-off in a fruit-filled trance.
Jokes about sweetness make us prance,
In this harvest, all enhance.

The night unfolds with a fruity twist,
Moments sweeter than we could list.
We'll toast to joy, oh how we've missed,
Autumn's charm, you can't resist!

In Search of Lost Flavors

Searching high and searching low,
For fruits that dance and put on a show.
Pears in pocket, ready to go,
Lost in laughter, stealing the glow.

Beneath the branches, oh what a scene,
Fruits in jester hats, quite the routine.
We've mused on each taste, so keen,
A fruity delight, makes hearts serene.

With fellow pickers, we craft and scheme,
Chasing tastes that make us beam.
Jokes passed around like a dream,
In our harvest, it's a scrumptious team.

On this quest, we find the prize,
Each flavor hidden, oh what a surprise!
In every bite, joy multiplies,
A feast of laughter under sunny skies!

Solstice Treasure of Sweetness

When the solstice sun is at its peak,
Fruits are tickled, their skins are sleek.
A pear on a skateboard, let's take a peek,
Rolling down hills, playing hide-and-seek.

A treasure of sweetness awaits us here,
With every crunch, we shed a tear.
Lemons dance, while rosy pears cheer,
Creating giggles, let's draw near.

Scooping up jests with ripe delight,
Taking juicy bites with all our might.
The fruit party gleams, oh what a sight,
In this solstice bash, our hearts ignite!

So raise your glass to playful cheer,
With fruits around, there's nothing to fear.
Laughter echoes, the end is clear,
In this treasure, friendship's near!

Nature's Golden Embrace

In the garden, fruits take a stand,
Golden globes, so sweet, so grand.
Laughing bees buzz with delight,
Dancing round till the fall of night.

Leaves whisper secrets, a cheeky tease,
Nudging fruits, swaying in the breeze.
A squirrel peeks with a twinkling eye,
Plotting schemes for a fruity pie.

Sunlight sprinkles warmth like confetti,
Birds chirp loud, oh so petty!
The clouds giggle as shadows play,
In this orchard of funny ballet.

Laughter ripens with each passing day,
As nature shows off her sassy display.
So come, partake in this joyful jest,
In golden embrace, we're truly blessed.

Echoes of Enchantment in the Orchard

Beneath the branches, where shadows creep,
Fruits hold secrets they plan to keep.
A parrot squawks with a witty quirk,
While rabbits plot their fruity work.

In a corner, a gnome takes a nap,
Dreaming of nectar and a frothy sap.
With a wink and nod, he joins the fun,
As apples tumble, one by one.

Cherries giggle in a rosy hue,
While pumpkins roll in a costume too.
The sun beams down, tickling all,
Nature's laughter, a joyful call.

Oh, the joy hidden in lush delight,
In this enchanted, silly sight.
With each step, find laughter anew,
In the orchard, the magic's true.

The Allure of Ripening Yonder

Over there, a fruit stands bright,
Winking at you in the golden light.
Figs and grapes, a motley crew,
Plotting mischief, oh what a view!

The wind whispers jokes as it blows,
Tickling the branches, where laughter grows.
Stumbling bumblebees, with silly flair,
Buzz around like they haven't a care.

Just beyond, of secrets they speak,
With twirling vines that resemble a sneak.
Oh, the peaches are plotting a parry,
As a sprightly fox sneaks with a cherry.

Witty banter fills the grassy glade,
As ripening fruit starts its parade.
Join in the fun, become a fan,
Of this merry plot, nature's grand plan.

The Joy Hidden in Abundance

In the fray of foliage so lush,
Citrus fruits join in the rush.
With zesty giggles, they all compete,
For the title of juiciest treat.

A cake is baking, a cheeky delight,
Using lemons that shine so bright.
While blueberries bounce like little balls,
The laughter echoes, as joy enthralls.

Bananas slide in a funny race,
While grapes chuckle at the silly pace.
The sweetness of life, so rich and round,
In abundance, the joy is found.

Come, indulge in this ripe parade,
Where every fruit's a prankster made.
In nature's pantry, with friends so true,
The joy of abundance is waiting for you.

Secrets in the Shadows of Trees

In the shade where secrets hide,
Whispers of squirrels and foxes collide.
A frisky breeze plays hide-and-seek,
As acorns drop, what a funny technique!

The wise old owl lets out a chuckle,
While raccoons dance with a playful shuffle.
Branches sway, a comical show,
As critters prepare for the grand tree row.

Beneath the leaves, treasures are found,
Pinecones like hats spin round and round.
A mischievous crow steals the limelight,
Cracking jokes while taking flight!

In the depths of green, sing-song delight,
Each creature's antics a sheer delight.
The shadows hold laughter, oh so bright,
With nature's comedy taking flight!

The Hidden Feast of Flora

Oh, the flowers conspire at dusk,
Throwing a party, oh, what a husk!
Petals giggle under the moon's gleam,
As bees waltz in a honeyed dream.

A table of blooms, a buffet so fine,
Dandelions sip on sweet sunshine.
While daisies twist in a leafy jig,
Rosebuds laugh, oh, look at them dig!

With a pinch of pollen and a splash of rain,
The night unfolds like a lively train.
Caterpillars munch, grow bigger with glee,
While ladybugs play hide-and-seek with a bee!

Posies gossip, sharing tales of delight,
As fireflies twinkle, glowing bright.
This hidden feast, oh what a show,
Nature's jesters, stealing the glow!

Nectar Streams and Luminous Dreams

In nectar rivers where giggles flow,
Bumblebees buzz with a comedic show.
Every flower a tiny stage,
Ladybugs perform with endless rage.

Moths in tuxedos flutter in flight,
Bright as stars in the velvety night.
Their dance routines spark laughter and fun,
As fireflies twinkle, one by one!

Waves of petals drift with a tease,
Caught in a whirl, oh, such a breeze!
Ants march in line, a silly parade,
Carrying crumbs, in a cascade!

Laughter bubbles in every bloom,
As nature's cast fills up the room.
In this realm where dreams run wild,
Even the sunbeam's a playful child!

Fruits of Reflection

Oh, the fruits of thought in the orchard sway,
Contemplating whether to play or stay.
Apples gossip, "Who's the juiciest crew?"
While pears nod, "Let's create a brew!"

Bananas slip into jokes, a slippery twist,
"Hold on tight!" they all insist.
Grapes in clusters chuckle and cling,
"Sours can't join; they spoil the spring!"

Peaches share tales of summer delight,
As oranges squirt with all their might.
Pineapples wear crowns, feeling so grand,
Joking they're royalty in fruitland!

In these orchards of humor, laughter's rife,
As fruits reflect on the joy of life.
With every chuckle, their spirits ascend,
In nature's buffet, the fun never ends!

In the Cradle of Nature's Gifts

In the orchard where laughter flies,
Fruits hide under leafy disguise.
Squirrels dance with cheeky grins,
While birds chirp tales of hapless sins.

With each pluck, visions unroll,
Sweetness bursts, a sugary soul.
The grass tickles our bare feet,
As giggles rise, oh what a treat!

Wobbling over the crunching ground,
The juiciest prize can be found.
With faces smeared in sticky bliss,
Who knew nature could be like this?

Once bitten, stories take flight,
In the realm of orchard delight.
Each harvest, a comic tale unfolds,
In the sunshine, both bright and bold.

A Hidden Harvest of Memories

Beneath the branches, oh what fun!
Chasing shadows, we all run.
A hidden treasure, just one more,
Buried laughter, behind nature's door.

Who knew fruit could be so sly?
With soft whispers, it passes by.
With sticky fingers, we recount,
The tales of sweetness, all amount.

Beware the bees, they hover near,
Invaders on our giggling cheer.
Yet we dance, twirl with zest,
Nature's bounty, truly blessed!

Old trees chuckle as we feast,
No greater joy, to say the least.
In our hearts, the laughter stays,
Harvesting memories in silly ways.

Secrets Woven into the Vine

Tangled roots and playful vines,
Whisper secrets through the pines.
With every twist, a joke appears,
Nature's laughter, music to ears.

Grapes giggle as they hang low,
Chortling tales we'll never know.
A clumsy stumble, a hop and skip,
Catching life's sweetest little quip.

Each fruit may hold a lively tale,
Of picnics grand and silly flail.
We sip juice from the silly past,
Cheers to moments that forever last!

In nature's web, fun's interlaced,
With every savor, we embrace.
Woven memories, time-friendly and bright,
Oh, what a blissful, joyful sight!

Fragile Moments of Harvest's Sweetness

In the dusk where shadows blend,
We gather treasures, fruits to lend.
With buckets full of giggles, we run,
Harvesting sweetness, oh what fun!

A stumble here, a laugh goes wild,
Even nature rocks, just like a child.
With every taste, the giggles flow,
In the orchard, the joy does grow.

The juice drips down from our chins,
As mischief dances, adventure begins.
Fragile moments, easy to break,
But laughter lingers, for friendship's sake.

Yes, every bite brings back the spark,
Filling our hearts, igniting the dark.
In these moments, we all partake,
Finding joy in the fruity quake!

Fruitful Secrets Beneath the Leaves

In the garden's embrace, something jives,
Mischief brews as the fruitiness thrives.
Fruits dressed up in a leafy disguise,
Giggles erupt as they catch our eyes.

A sneaky bite brings a grin so wide,
Wild flavors dance, no need to hide.
Nature's prank as we munch with glee,
A treasure hunt in the wild, carefree.

Juicy whispers in the shade do play,
Some fruits have jokes that simply slay.
Under the boughs, we giggle and shout,
What a surprise, there's much to tout!

So let's pluck the joy with laughter here,
Secret flavors we hold so dear.
In our fruity fun, we are all the same,
For laughter is the sweetest game!

Hidden Gems in a Garden's Heart

In the garden's nook, treasures lie,
With laughter and glee, oh me, oh my!
Colors pop like a vibrant cage,
Each fruit a story, a comic page.

Beneath the leaves where the giggles swirl,
Juicy secrets start to unfurl.
A pink thing winks, a sneaky jest,
Gather 'round, it's a fruit-finding fest!

Tickle your taste buds, take a chance,
Here, fruits break out in a silly dance.
Who knew such gems were hid away,
In laughter's grip, we joyfully sway!

So grab a basket, come join the fun,
With nature's humor, we're never done.
Petals chuckle, and fruits share a song,
In this garden, we all belong!

Sweet Delights of Nature's Bounty

Oh, the treats that dangle so spry,
Nature's candy, no need to lie.
Round and plump, they tease and taunt,
With every bite, the flavors flaunt.

In a riot of colors, they giggle loud,
As we reach for them, feeling proud.
Honeyed whispers float on the breeze,
Nature's jest, it's a fruity tease!

Juicy chuckles burst with delight,
Every nibble feels just right.
From twinkling apples to mischief's pear,
It's a sweet parade everywhere!

So let's delight in nature's jest,
In her playful hands, we feel blessed.
With laughter as ripe as the sweetest fruit,
We savor the fun, oh what a hoot!

The Hidden Splendor of Harvested Joy

In the dusk of day, the wild birds sing,
Harvested joy is a curious thing.
Underfoot, the ground is a canvas bright,
Fruits play hide and seek in the fading light.

A chuckling bunch of grapes on the vine,
Whispering secrets, oh how divine!
Every crunch brings a joyful cheer,
Nature's laughter is drawing near.

Beneath the branches where mischief waits,
Fruits with antics behind the gates.
Pick them gently, with a wink and a grin,
For in every bite, the laughter begins!

So gather 'round, let's feast and play,
As nature smiles in her own quirky way.
With joy on our lips, let the fun unfold,
In the treasures found, our stories told!

Fragrant Delights of the Grove

In the grove where laughter grows,
Sweet scents dance where sunlight flows.
Round and plump, they hide in shade,
Whispering secrets, in games well played.

Bouncing squirrels join the fun,
Chasing shadows, on the run.
Jokes are ripe upon each branch,
As breezes come to join the dance.

With giggles sprouting up nearby,
Each juicy gem makes spirits fly.
Nature's comedy, oh what a sight,
As fruity treasures spark delight.

In the grove, oh what a place,
Where nature wears a funny face.
Pick your laughter, take a seat,
For here, the joy is ripe and sweet.

Nature's Velvet Surprise

In the garden where mischief plays,
Soft green whispers fill the days.
A hidden trove, the fruits await,
Soft and smooth, they tempt your fate.

Beneath the leaves, they giggle loud,
"Pick us quick!" they call, so proud.
What's this game of hide and seek?
Each round globe, a treasure peak!

The bees buzz in their buzzing spree,
"Come and taste!" they sing with glee.
Laughter spills from every vine,
As golden drops of joy entwine.

Have a nibble, share a grin,
In this patch, we all can win!
Nature's prank, both sly and sweet,
Turns each moment into a treat.

Buried in the Blossoms

Among the blooms, a treasure lies,
Covered well from curious eyes.
With petals dancing in the breeze,
Jesters hidden among the trees.

Round and plump, a playful jest,
Nature's bounty, a funny quest.
"Dig a little!" they tease and play,
Gems of laughter on display.

With every pluck, a giggle bursts,
Fruity joy that never thirsts.
Why so shy? Come join the cheer,
Each surprise is waiting here!

In blossoms bright, the fun's alive,
Where sweetness reigns and jokes arrive.
Uncovering joy on every stalk,
A comedy show among the flock.

The Allure of Sunlit Spheres

Bright orbs dangle, gleaming round,
Under sunshine, they bounce around.
A playful wink from nature's hand,
Inviting all to join the band.

Giggles echo in the fields,
Ripe with laughter, joy it yields.
Each tempting sphere says, "Take a bite!"
As shadows dance in pure delight.

Squeezed in laughter, juices flow,
Nature's charm, a vibrant show.
Rolling 'round as if to tease,
And tickle hearts with playful ease.

From golden hues to shades of green,
These cheeky globes keep smiles keen.
In the garden, it's plain to see,
Life's a jest, come laugh with me!

The Dance of Sun-Kissed Delights

In the orchard, laughter rings,
Fruit flies dance, oh what fun!
Bouncing off with jiggly wings,
Chasing sunlight, one by one.

Lemon's sour face gives a smirk,
While apples roll, they think they're slick.
Bananas slip with a little quirk,
In this waltz of fruity trick!

Grapes giggle as they tumble down,
Playing hide and seek with bees.
Cherries blush, they spin around,
While pears just hang from leafy trees.

Together they flaunt colorful flair,
All in sync, their fruity tease.
Nature's party, without a care,
Join the fun, just feel the breeze!

Tales from Beneath the Canopy.

Underneath the leafy spread,
Squirrels plot in a hushed tone.
Whispers of snacks fill up their head,
Turns out they're stealing my scone!

A spider spins tales of delight,
Of raindrops and the sun's warm glow.
"Watch your step!" is heard in fright,
When worms perform their dance below.

Beneath the boughs, the shadows creep,
Mice debate whose cheese is best.
Each secret made is theirs to keep,
A nutty feast, they never rest!

As dusk descends, the stories swell,
Laughter echoes, rippling glee.
In this green theater, all is well,
Every critter's a star, you see!

Golden Harvest of Secrets

Glimmers of gold hang from the vine,
Giggling birds sing sweet and clear.
"Which fruit's finest? Come, let's dine!"
Ripe jokes spread, laughter is near.

On windy days, the apples tease,
Rolling down for a comical show.
Oranges bounce with perfect ease,
While puns fly high, faster they go!

Amongst the leaves, the chatter grows,
"What's worse than a bad fruit pun?"
"A lame joke!" the grape stands close,
As everyone bursts with fun!

With baskets full, each picks their prize,
Giggles squish between cheeks so wide.
Here laughter adds flavor to pies,
A harvest shared, joy worldwide!

Orchard Whispers at Dusk

As sunset paints the sky with cheer,
Crickets start their chirpy tales.
Breezy whispers twist and veer,
Over pathways where joy prevails.

Frogs in ponds croak jokes so sly,
While berries blush, hiding their glee.
"Why did the grape refuse to fly?"
"Because it couldn't find a tree!"

Mice frolic near the pumpkin patch,
Bouncing off leaves with a squeaky cheer.
Squirrels plot to make a snatch,
But end up tangled, oh dear, oh dear!

In the evening's soft embrace,
Each creature shares a happy bite.
Laughter lingers in this place,
Orchard dreams dance into the night!

A Canvas of Green and Gold

In a garden where laughter grows,
A fruit with a grin, nobody knows.
Leaves whisper secrets, tales untold,
Under sunlight, a sight to behold.

With a twirl and a jig, it dances free,
Swinging from branches, as happy as can be.
Each bite's a giggle, sweet to the core,
Who knew a fruit could be so much more?

Squirrels gather, thieving with glee,
Trying to snatch what's meant for me.
But I laugh as they dart, take a big leap,
That fruity delight, my secret to keep.

When the harvest arrives, it's quite the show,
A fruity parade with gusto and glow.
We'll toast with a chuckle, my friends and I,
To the merry fruit that makes our hearts fly.

The Enchantment of Orchard Shadows

In orchards where shadows play tag,
A quirky fruit wears a silly rag.
With a spunky veneer and a smile so wide,
It charms all the critters that frolic inside.

The sun spills laughter upon every branch,
While the chattering birds begin their dance.
Each crunch is a belly laugh, sweet and bright,
A juicy delight that feels just right.

Whispers of mischief among the leaves,
As playful bugs craft their silly weaves.
They wiggle and giggle, a circus of cheer,
While the fruit watches on, full of good cheer.

So here's to the fun found beneath the sun,
Where every day is goofy, every laugh is spun.
With oh-so-funny delights up on high,
In the enchanted orchard, where humor won't die.

Echoes of the Abundant Orchard

In echoes where giggles float through the air,
A fruit's tale unfolds with whimsical flair.
It jests with the breeze, tickles the trees,
As it shares all its jokes with a chorus of bees.

Round and plump, with a wink in its skin,
It plays peek-a-boo with each tasty grin.
With each little bite, joy fills the void,
Oh, the laughter it brings is never destroyed.

The ground is a carpet of colors to find,
Where wonders and jests are beautifully intertwined.
Laughter erupts in this vibrant frolic,
A sweet symphony, playful and colic.

So gather around for a raucous delight,
In the garden of grins, where the day's ever bright.
For in every cheerful munch and every slight,
Is a festival of flavor, merry and light.

Beneath the Lush Canopy

Beneath leafy arches where smiles reside,
A wonderful fruit takes a tiptoeing stride.
With each playful bounce, it jests and it jives,
Thriving amidst giggles, oh how it thrives!

The chubby clouds join in, fluffy and white,
Dancing with rays of the warm, golden light.
As squirrels throw parties, the raccoons all cheer,
A carnival atmosphere fills with good cheer.

From grinning tree trunks, jokes are exchanged,
Teasing the rabbits, they feel so deranged.
All gather round under skies painted blue,
To witness the wonders of the fruity debut.

So come to the orchard, where joy takes its mark,
In this whimsical haven, life's bright and stark.
A laughter-filled garden, our favorite place,
Where each delicious bite brings a smile to our face.

Wisps of Autumn's Lament

In fields of gold, the critters dance,
Chasing leaves in a silly prance.
Squirrels hide nuts like they're on a spree,
While rabbits plot to join the jubilee.

With apples grinning from every branch,
The pumpkins tease with a cheeky ranch.
A scarecrow winks with a rusty smile,
As crows play tag, just for a while.

The breeze giggles through the turning trees,
As nature teases on a playful breeze.
The dusk is painted in hues of fun,
With shadows frolicking, we're never done.

Tapestry of Nature's Gifts

A curious cat in a quilted coat,
Chased a fluttering insect, a noble goat.
Beneath the boughs, laughter rings,
As foxes juggle with silly things.

The daisies chuckle as they take a bow,
While butterflies gossip – oh, where and how?
A daffodil dons a tiny hat,
And on a snail, a jazz band sat!

Lemons giggle from their sunny perch,
While bees do the polka in a merry church.
Together they share some secret tea,
Every sip brings a fit of glee.

The Orchard's Silent Song

In the orchard's heart, mischief brews,
With giggling ghosts and dancing shoes.
A gathering of fruit, quite a sight,
Plotting adventures into the night.

An apple whispered to an eager pear,
"Let's sneak away, without a care!"
While grapes snickered, sharing a wink,
As bananas wore glasses, oh what a blink!

As moonlight drapes in a silk embrace,
The fruits embark on a wild chase.
With laughter echoing under the stars,
They swirled and twirled like rock stars.

Blossoms Abound

In fields of petals, laughter flies,
With bees wearing sunglasses, oh my, oh my!
A tulip tells jokes with a snazzy grin,
While daisies play tag, eager to win.

The wind, a jester, tickles the blooms,
While the sun plays peek-a-boo, adding to the tunes.
A ladybug dances, a diva so grand,
With a crew of ants forming a band.

Butterflies flutter as they sing duets,
Sharing grand tales, you bet, you bet!
With giggles and grins, the show won't cease,
Nature's zany circus, a sweet masterpiece.

Treasures Hidden

Digging through soil with a cheeky grin,
For sparkling gems, let the fun begin!
Critters all chatter, plotting a scheme,
As worms join in for the treasure dream.

"Finders keepers!" exclaims a bold crow,
While earthworms wiggle below, moving slow.
Golden acorns and shiny stones,
In nature's wallet, all alone.

The laughter rings out as friends unite,
In search of riches, oh what a sight!
With treasures of goodies and giggles to share,
In the heart of the woods, none can compare.

Whispers of Orchard Legends

In the orchard, giggles bloom,
Apples dance to chase the gloom.
A quirky squirrel with a hat,
Sings to Mr. Chubby Cat.

The birds gossip in the trees,
About a fruit that sways in breeze.
A crazy story, wild and bright,
Of secret feasts that last all night.

The farmer laughs, what a sight!
As two rabbits start a fight.
Over the fruit, they both adore,
But it rolls away, oh what a score!

Now legend spreads of tasty finds,
With tales of treasure left behind.
Each fruit a gem, quite absurd,
In whispers shared, not heard, just heard.

A Feast of Colors and Flavors

In a bowl of colors bright,
A fruit parade brings pure delight.
Yellow, green, and rosy red,
A salad bar where dreams are fed.

Cherries giggle, lemons frown,
Dancing fruits do wear a crown.
Bananas flip, they like to slide,
Mangoes waltz with silly pride.

Every taste a burst of cheer,
Ripe laughter ripens in the sphere.
A feast that tickles every tongue,
A merry song of fruit is sung.

When friends arrive, it's such a blast,
With juicy jokes and flavors vast.
A spread so bright, you'll surely see,
Nature's humor, wild and free!

Tales Told in the Rustling Leaves

In the trees, the whispers play,
Leaves tell stories every day.
Of cheeky mice that steal a treat,
And parties held with all the sweets.

The branches sway and giggles rise,
As winds carry the clever lies.
A tale of fruits that wear a coat,
Of silk and sparkles, they gloat, they float.

Oh, silly tales of sticky hands,
Of wild adventures in far-off lands.
The orchard sings with laughter bright,
As leaves play tricks in morning light.

So listen close, and you might find,
The stories told are quite unlined.
With humor woven in each breeze,
Oh, nature's jokes, designed to tease!

In Search of Nature's Hidden Gold

A treasure hunt beneath the sun,
With friends, we laugh and start the fun.
A shiny clue, oh what a sight,
Leads us running, hearts so light.

Under trees with leafy shades,
We dig and dance through sunny glades.
A treasure map made out of snack,
Leads to treasure, and no lack!

A bouncing berry rolls away,
We chase it down, oh what a play!
Who knew gold could be so sweet,
In nature's game that can't be beat?

With giggles loud, and smiles so wide,
We find our treasure, friends beside.
In every fruit, a secret gleams,
Nature's riches are our dreams!

Treasures Ripening in Gentle Light

In the garden, fruits so round,
Dancing lightly on the ground.
Chasing shadows, game of catch,
Among the leaves, we find our match.

Golden globes all in a row,
They giggle as the breezes blow.
Laughter rings, it's quite a sight,
Sneaking bites, oh what delight!

See the bees in suits so bright,
Buzzing 'round their sweet invite.
Sticky fingers, playful mess,
Nature's candy, we confess!

Bouncing, prancing, purest glee,
Underneath the old oak tree.
In this treasure hunt we play,
Fruits of joy, we seize the day!

A Tapestry of Juicy Wonders

Under sun, we weave our dreams,
With laughter sweet as citrus creams.
Fruits hang low, a playful tease,
Tickling noses in the breeze.

One little fruit, so round and bright,
Calls to us, "Come take a bite!"
It rolls away with cheeky glee,
Chasing it is fun, you see!

Patchwork colors, oh so bold,
In nature's quilt of green and gold.
Each luscious orb holds a surprise,
Droplets of sunshine in their eyes.

Gather 'round, let stories flow,
Of battles fought with juice and glow.
With every snack, the giggles grow,
In this wonderland, we steal the show!

Glimpses of Gold in the Green

In a field of emerald grass,
Golden orbs of joy, they pass.
Like tiny suns, they wink and grin,
A merry chase about to begin!

Swinging baskets, laughter loud,
Among the fruits, we're feeling proud.
A cheeky squirrel throws a show,
Stealing snacks, he steals the glow.

A sneak attack, a juicy fight,
Splashing juice in pure delight.
With sticky hands and silly grins,
This fruity war, it's where it wins!

Under skies with fluffy clouds,
We're the giggling, silly crowds.
A treasure hunt that never ends,
In fruity fields, we make amends.

Nature's Lullaby of Abundance

Whispers soft in the orchard bright,
Nature hums with pure delight.
Pondering fruits, they sway and swing,
Like bouncy balls, they leap and cling.

A crow joins in, with caw and hop,
Stealing snacks, he just won't stop!
Dancing leaves, oh what a tease,
Sharing bites beneath the trees.

Juicy secrets wrapped in skin,
With every munch, a playful sin.
Our picnic spreads with laughs and cheer,
A treasure hunt that draws us near.

As stars peek through, we sigh with glee,
What a day in nature's spree!
With giggles shared and stories spun,
In this bounty, we've surely won!

Lustrous Orbs of Pleasures

In a garden bright and fair,
Lustrous orbs hang in the air.
Plump and juicy, yellow-green,
Winking at us, what a scene!

Sliced them up, a merry fate,
With a grin, we can't wait.
Bobbing heads and silly grins,
Choosing favorites, oh what sins!

Jesters in a fruity spree,
Juicy jokes and laughter free.
With every bite, a giggle grows,
To the dance of juicy shows!

As we feast, our hearts take flight,
In this bounty, pure delight.
Lustrous orbs send us to cheer,
Grab a slice and join the cheer!

Hidden Splendor in Every Bite

A secret stash beneath the leaves,
Nature's gift that never deceives.
Beneath the skin, a treasure waits,
With every crunch, it laughs and baits.

A fruity giggle in the air,
Who knew that bliss could sing and share?
Chomping down, a burst of joy,
Sweet or tart, what a ploy!

A golden slice, a splendid bite,
We dance around with pure delight.
With friends in tow, we'll take our chance,
To munch and crunch in fruity dance!

From tree to tummy, such a ride,
With hidden splendor, joy won't hide.
So pluck a piece, give it a whirl,
Taste the laughter, let it twirl!

Nature's Well-Kept Secrets

In the orchard, whispers sing,
Nature's gems, oh what they bring!
Secrets held in juicy skin,
With bites of laughter, let's begin.

A slice revealed, the crowd astonished,
Juicy giggles leave us astonished.
Who knew such fun could hide away,
In golden globes, bright as the day?

Dancers of the grove, take heed,
With every chew, we joyfully lead.
Nature's whispers tickle our ears,
As flavor bursts ignite our cheers!

So chase the stash behind the leaves,
Trust in joy that nature weaves.
With every bite, our spirits soar,
Nature's secrets, we'll explore!

Whispers of Golden Harvest

Gather 'round, come take a seat,
For whispers fill the air, so sweet.
A golden harvest on display,
With every nibble, we laugh away!

Chubby fingers reach so sly,
Who could resist? Oh my, oh my!
Juicy wonders, one and all,
Fall on laughter as we call.

With every slice, a joke unfolds,
Stories shared, as taste, it molds.
In every giggle, joy we find,
Golden harvest, one of a kind!

So raise a toast to fruits so fine,
With every fruity bite, we shine.
Whispers linger, let them spread,
Joyful treasures to be fed!